Prager University ("PragerU") is redefining how people think about media and education. Watched millions of times every day, PragerU is the world's leading educational nonprofit focused on changing minds through the creative use of digital media. From intellectual, fact-based 5-Minute Videos and powerful personal storytelling to educational animated shows made just for kids—PragerU helps people of all ages discover and keep pro-American values.

PragerU Kids offers edu-tainment (educational and entertaining content) across the K-12th grade spectrum. With kids shows, cartoons, and literature that teach history, life skills, and character building in an age-appropriate manner, PragerU Kids offers content that parents trust and children love. Watch for free and learn more at PragerUkids.com.

Published by PragerU

15021 Ventura Boulevard #552

Sherman Oaks, CA 91403

WELCOME TO STREET SMARTS CIVICS EDITION!

This workbook is designed to accompany you for each video lesson and enhance your understanding of American Civics. With engaging activities and thought-provoking exercises, you can explore new concepts and expand your knowledge in a fun and interactive way. Let's join Uncle Sam and put our civics street smarts to the test!

Topic Overview: This section outlines the topic of the video and gives all of the necessary background information and key concepts.

Fun Fact: Along the way, we'll learn important quotes and fun facts about the topic. This section highlights these points of interest.

Fill-in-the-Blank: The fill-in-the-blank worksheet helps you follow the video episode and stay engaged with the lesson. Pay attention and try to find the answers from the show. Or, your teacher may want you to try it on your own to see what you know or have learned.

Writing: The writing page is a great space to gather your thoughts, reflect, and express what you saw, heard, or thought. Your teacher may have specific instructions here, so listen up! If not, this can be a space to capture everything you learned.

Check your answers with the answer key at the end of each section to see how you did!

TABLE OF CONTENTS

THE DECLARATION OF
INDEPENDENCE

scan here
to watch
this episode

THE DECLARATION OF
INDEPENDENCE

The Declaration of Independence was a landmark document completely unique to the United States of America. It spelled out three things:

Principles for good government, how King George the Third's oppressive rule did not measure up to that standard, and a formal declaration of the 13 colonies' independence from Great Britain.

In today's episode, we learned that the Declaration of Independence was originally drafted by Thomas Jefferson and adopted by the Continental Congress on July 4th, 1776. The introductory statement—including the Preamble—announced the creation of a new country and proclaimed that all persons are created equal and have three unalienable rights: Life, Liberty and the Pursuit of Happiness. Our Founding Fathers literally wanted us to be happy and free.

FUN FACT:

The first person to sign the declaration was John Hancock. His signature was so fancy and large, that we still use his name to ask people for their signature today!

THE DECLARATION OF
INDEPENDENCE

1 Adopted on _____ , the Declaration of Independence was the founding document of the United States of America that established what a government's role should be, explained how King George III's rule did not measure up to that standard, and officially declared the nation independent from Great Britain.

2 Cited grievances against _____ of Great Britain

3 The introductory section of the Declaration includes the _____ , which stated that

4 Power is derived from the _____

5 Cited three inalienable rights: ____ , ____ AND THE ____

6 Originally drafted by _____ who became the 3rd President

7 Adopted by the Continental Congress on _____

8 The first person to sign the declaration was _____

John Hancock

9 Declared that all persons are created _____

THE DECLARATION OF
INDEPENDENCE

_____

_____

_____

_____

_____

_____

_____

_____

_____

_____

_____

_____

_____

_____

_____

_____

_____

_____

_____

_____

_____

_____

Answer Key:

1: July 4, 1776   **2:** King George, III   **3:** Preamble   **4:** Consent of the Governed   **5:** Life, Liberty and the Pursuit of Happiness

6: Thomas Jefferson   **7:** July 4th, 1776   **8:** John Hancock   **9:** Equal

CONSTITUTION

scan here
to watch
this episode

CONSTITUTION

The Constitution was written by several of the Founding Fathers in 1787, including James Madison, who is known as the "Father of the Constitution." It became the supreme law of the land when nine of the original 13 states ratified it in 1788.

The Constitution, with its original seven Articles, establishes the federal government's structure. While this important document gives the federal government certain powers like levying taxes, coining money, and declaring war, it also ensures that those powers are limited and respects the rights of the people and state and local governments.

Our Founding Fathers hoped future generations would preserve the key principles of the Constitution, but they also recognized the need for modifications both then and in the future.

This is why they allowed for changes to be made to it, called amendments, and as of 2022, there have been a total of 27 amendments.

CONSTITUTION

In today's episode, we learned that the Constitution is the document that created the governing principles of the United States that are still in effect today. We also learned that it establishes separation of powers, also known as "Checks and Balances," by creating three branches of government: Legislative, Executive, and Judicial.

Finally, we learned that the first 10 amendments ratified in 1791 to the Constitution are called the Bill of Rights.

FUN FACT:

Rhode Island was the last of the original 13 states to ratify the Constitution in May of 1790.

CONSTITUTION

Written in 1787, the U.S. Constitution, with its 7 original Articles, establishes the structure of the federal government.

1 The first part of the Constitution, called the Preamble, begins with the phrase "We the _____."

2 _____ is known as the "Father of the Constitution."

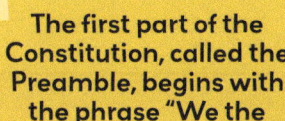

3 The Constitution created the Legislative, Executive, and Judicial branches to separate the powers of the government, a system commonly known as "Checks and _____."

4 The Constitution grants Congress abilities to levy taxes, coin money, and _____.

7 It took _____ states to originally ratify the Constitution from 1787 to 1788.

5 _____ is the term used to describe a change to the Constitution.

6 Ratified in 1791, _____ is the name of the first 10 amendments to the Constitution.

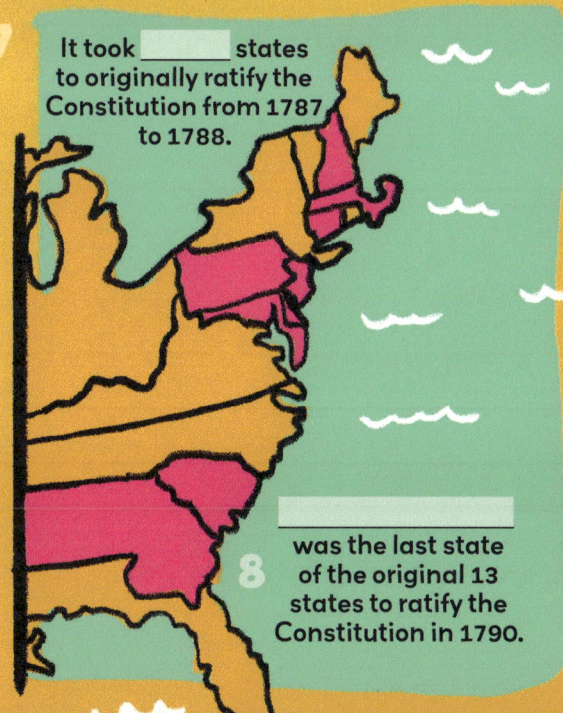

8 _____ was the last state of the original 13 states to ratify the Constitution in 1790.

CONSTITUTION

This is the part where you get to write something about what you learned, saw, heard, or thought; so grab that pen and get going!

_____

_____

_____

_____

_____

_____

_____

_____

_____

_____

_____

_____

_____

_____

_____

_____

_____

_____

_____

_____

_____

Answer Key:

1: People   **2:** James Madison   **3:** Balances   **4:** Declare War   **5:** Amendment   **6:** The Bill of Rights   **7:** Nine   **8:** Rhode Island

BILL OF RIGHTS

scan here
to watch
this episode

10

THE BILL OF RIGHTS

The Bill of Rights was drafted and proposed by James Madison in 1789. It was created because some of the Founding Fathers felt that the Constitution gave too much power to the federal government. It guarantees personal freedoms for American citizens, like freedom of speech and religion. It also limits the powers of the federal government and asserts that powers not delegated to Congress are reserved to the individual states and to the people.

The Bill of Rights is the first 10 amendments to the U.S. Constitution.

The 1st Amendment guarantees the right to freedom of speech, to the free exercise of religion and of the press, and the 2nd Amendment guarantees the right to bear arms. The 3rd Amendment prohibits the government from housing soldiers without a person's consent in times of peace, and the 4th Amendment prohibits the search and seizure of private property by the government without good reason.

THE BILL OF RIGHTS

The 5th Amendment protects citizens from being tried twice for the same crime and incriminating themselves, while the 6th guarantees the right to a speedy and public trial. The 7th guarantees that those accused of a crime in a civil lawsuit have a right to a trial by jury, and the 8th protects against cruel and unusual punishments. The 9th Amendment states that the people may have rights not listed in the Constitution. And finally, the 10th Amendment expresses that powers not explicitly given in the Constitution to the federal government are reserved to the people and the states.

The Bill of Rights was and still is essential for protecting many freedoms that we still enjoy today.

FUN FACT:

Though the phrase "Separation of Church and State" is a phrase commonly associated with the 1st Amendment, it's not actually in the Constitution! The term was actually pulled from a letter from Thomas Jefferson to the Danbury Baptist Association of Connecticut in 1802.

THE BILL OF RIGHTS

Proposed by James Madison in 1789, the Bill of Rights was originally created because many states felt the U.S. Constitution gave too much power to the _____ government. The Founders created the Bill of Rights to protect our freedoms. The Bill of Rights are the first ____ amendments to the Constitution.

3 The First Amendment protects the right to say what you want freely, known as Freedom of _____, freedom of religion and the press, and the right to assemble and petition the government.

The Ninth Amendment states that the people may have other rights not listed in the Constitution.

6 The Second Amendment guarantees citizens the fundamental right to keep and bear _____.

The Third Amendment prevents the government from forcing the people to house soldiers without their consent.

5 The _____ Amendment protects people from being tried twice for the same crime and incriminating themselves, and ensures a fair legal process for all citizens.

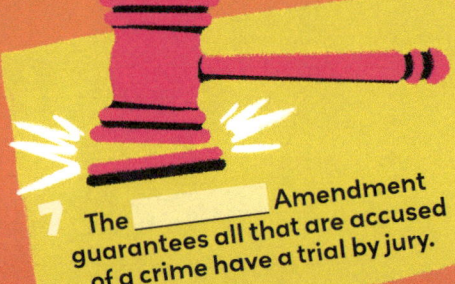

7 The _____ Amendment guarantees all that are accused of a crime have a trial by jury.

The Eighth Amendment protects against cruel and unusual punishments, including excessive bail.

4 The Sixth Amendment guarantees that someone accused of a crime has the right to a speedy and public _____.

The Fourth Amendment prevents the government from searching through and taking your property without a good reason.

8 The _____ Amendment ensures that any power not expressly given to the federal government in the Constitution is reserved to the people and individual states.

THE BILL OF RIGHTS

This is the part where you get to write something about what you learned, saw, heard, or thought; so grab that pen and get going!

_____

_____

_____

_____

_____

_____

_____

_____

_____

_____

_____

_____

_____

_____

_____

_____

_____

_____

_____

_____

_____

_____

_____

Answer Key:
1: Federal   **2:** Ten   **3:** Speech   **4:** Trial   **5:** Fifth   **6:** Arms   **7:** Seventh   **8:** Tenth

EXECUTIVE BRANCH

scan here
to watch
this episode

EXECUTIVE BRANCH

The United States Constitution divides the federal government into three different branches: Executive, Legislative, and Judicial. The reason the Founding Fathers did this was to create a system of checks and balances so that political power would not be concentrated in any one single person or group.

The Founders feared that if any one branch or individual had too much power, this would threaten the freedom of the American people. If that happened, they worried the United States would become a dictatorship like other countries.

In today's episode, we learned that the Executive Branch is led by the president, whose main responsibility is to carry out and enforce laws. He is considered the leader of the country and oftentimes considered "the most powerful man in the world." In order to serve as president, a person must be a natural-born United States citizen, must be at least 35 years old, and must have lived in the United States for at least 14 years.

EXECUTIVE BRANCH

The Constitution gives the Electoral College the responsibility of electing the president. In addition to the president, the Executive Branch also includes the vice president and the Cabinet.

The Cabinet is composed of the president's most senior advisors—commonly referred to as secretaries—who oversee different departments, which include education, energy, defense, treasury, transportation, and more. They help the president with any problems he might face.

Additional duties of the president include: vetoing or signing bills into law, making treaties, and appointing justices, both of which have to be approved by a Senate vote. Lastly, the president also serves as the Commander in Chief, which puts him in charge of the military and overall military strategy.

FUN FACT:

The 22nd Amendment was ratified in 1951 and limits the president to being elected twice. Prior to its ratification, Franklin D. Roosevelt was the only president to be elected for more than two terms.

EXECUTIVE BRANCH

1 _____ leads the Executive Branch of U.S. Government. This person is the highest ranking government official in the United States. He is considered the leader of the country and, oftentimes, "the most powerful man in the world."

2 The Executive Branch is responsible for enforcing laws, appointing Supreme Court justices and ambassadors, and _____.

3 Once the president receives a bill from Congress, he can sign it into law, or he can _____ it, which means to reject it.

4 In order to serve as president, a person must have been a U.S. citizen since birth, have lived in the United States for at least 14 years, and be at least _____ years old.

5 The Executive Branch also includes the vice president as well as the president's _____, which is a group of trusted senior advisors who oversee different government departments.

6 Because the president "shall be Commander in Chief," he is in charge of the _____ and overall defense strategy.

8 The Constitution gives the _____ the responsibility of electing the president.

7 Ever since the 22nd Amendment was ratified in 1951, a president can serve a maximum of _____ 4-year terms.

9 _____ is the only president to have served more than two terms, which he did before the 22nd Amendment was ratified in 1951.

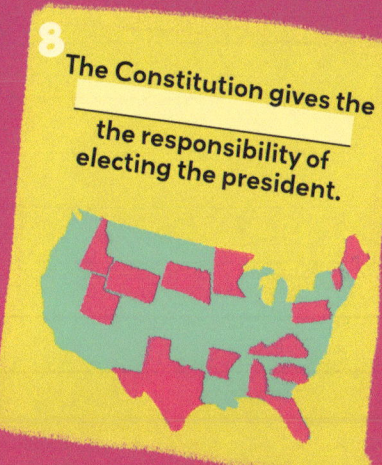

EXECUTIVE BRANCH

This is the part where you get to write something about what you learned, saw, heard, or thought; so grab that pen and get going!

_____
_____
_____
_____
_____
_____
_____
_____
_____
_____
_____
_____
_____
_____
_____
_____
_____
_____
_____
_____
_____

Answer Key:

1: The President **2:** Making Treaties **3:** Veto **4:** 35 **5:** Cabinet **6:** Military **7:** Two **8:** Electoral College **9:** Franklin Delano Roosevelt

JUDICIAL BRANCH

scan here
to watch
this episode

20

JUDICIAL BRANCH

In today's episode, we learned about the Judicial Branch, one of the three branches of the U.S. government established by the U.S. Constitution.

It comprises the federal court system, which includes district courts, appellate courts, and the highest court in the nation, the Supreme Court.

The Supreme Court, also known as the "court of last resort," is the final court of appeals.

The main purpose of the Court is to judge impartially in the event of a dispute about a law or the meaning of the Constitution, a process called "judicial review." The Supreme Court has nine justices, including the highest-ranking justice of the Supreme Court, the Chief Justice.

All federal judges are appointed by the president and confirmed by a simple majority of the Senate. Unlike the president and Congress, who are elected for terms for a certain number of years, Supreme Court justices serve for life (or until they retire or are impeached and removed from office). Since they don't run for election, they are protected from political pressure and public opinion and can rule independently on the meaning of laws.

We the People

JUDICIAL BRANCH

For a plaintiff, that is the party who initiates a lawsuit, to have their court case heard in a federal district court, the case has to meet certain criteria. These criteria include cases that involve issues with a federal law, with the U.S. Constitution, with the U.S. government, or with treaties. Most federal cases start out in one of the 94 federal district courts. If the plaintiff is unsatisfied with the resulting verdict, they can appeal to have their case heard in a circuit court. If the circuit court decides to hear the case and the plaintiff is still unsatisfied with the result, they can appeal to have their case heard by the Supreme Court.

The Supreme Court has the right to hear certain kinds of cases first; this is known as "original jurisdiction." These cases include those involving ambassadors, other officials, and the states.

The final verdict of a Supreme Court case sets a legal precedent for the U.S. in perpetuity unless later overturned by a subsequent Supreme Court ruling.

FUN FACT:

There has only ever been one Supreme Court justice who was impeached. In 1804, Samuel Chase was impeached by the House of Representatives, who charged him with acting improperly in cases and for having a political bias that impacted his rulings. He was later acquitted by the Senate in 1805.

JUDICIAL BRANCH

1 The Judicial Branch of the U.S. government comprises district courts, circuit courts, and the highest court in the nation, the _____ Court.

SUPREME COURT

CIRCUIT COURTS

DISTRICT COURTS

We the People

2 The highest ranking judge of the Supreme Court is the _____.

3 If the plaintiff, also known as the party who initiates a lawsuit, isn't satisfied with a verdict they can _____ to a higher court.

4 When people disagree about whether a law or government action is constitutional, the job of the Judicial Branch is to resolve the issue by interpreting the _____.

5 The ability federal and state courts have to determine if a law or action by the government is constitutional is known as _____.

6 All Supreme Court justices are appointed by the president and must be confirmed by a simple majority in the _____.

7 Supreme Court justices are appointed for _____.

8 The Supreme Court has "original jurisdiction," which is the right to be the first to hear a case. It has this jurisdiction for cases involving _____.

JUDICIAL BRANCH

This is the part where you get to write something about what you learned, saw, heard, or thought; so grab that pen and get going!

_____
_____
_____
_____
_____
_____
_____
_____
_____
_____
_____
_____
_____
_____
_____
_____
_____
_____
_____
_____
_____
_____
_____

Answer Key:
1: Supreme **2:** Chief Justice **3:** Appeal **4:** Constitution **5:** Judicial Review **6:** Senate **7:** Life **8:** 2 or More States

LEGISLATIVE BRANCH

scan here
to watch
this episode

LEGISLATIVE BRANCH

In today's episode, we learned about the Legislative Branch, one of the three branches of the U.S. government established by the U.S. Constitution. It's made up of two chambers, the Senate and the House of Representatives. Every state has exactly two senators, meaning that, altogether, the 50 states have a total of 100 senators. The number of representatives each state has is based on its population, and there are a total of 435 members of the House of Representatives.

The Legislative Branch's main job is to propose and pass bills into laws. These laws are very important because they govern the lives of every American.

This branch also has other responsibilities, such as confirming presidential nominations and, if necessary, declaring war. Anyone in the House and Senate can propose a bill, and after that, the members debate and vote on the bill. If it is approved by a majority of members in both chambers, it goes to the president, who has the choice to sign it into law. In the event that the president vetoes, or rejects, a proposed bill, it gets sent back to Congress. Congress can then override the veto and make the bill a law by a 2/3 majority vote in both the House and the Senate.

LEGISLATIVE BRANCH

The Framers of the Constitution divided the power of Congress between two houses to balance the interests of both the small and large states.

Senators represent their entire states, but members of the House represent individual districts. The Senate was intended to act more deliberately than the House, so their terms are six years as opposed to two years for the House of Representatives. Unlike the Executive Branch, members of the Legislative Branch have no term limits, meaning they can be re-elected an unlimited number of times.

FUN FACT:

In the event that a sitting president is believed to be guilty of misconduct, it is the House of Representatives that will vote to pass articles of impeachment, and if they are passed, it is the Senate that holds the trial that decides whether he or she is guilty.

LEGISLATIVE BRANCH

1 The Legislative Branch, which consists of the Senate and the House of Representatives, is collectively known as _____. Its main responsibility is to propose and pass bills into laws.

THE HOUSE OF REPRESENTATIVES

2 How many members a state has in the House of Representatives is determined by its _____. There are a total of 435 members.

3 The _____ presides over, or leads, the House of Representatives.

4 _____ has the power to pass articles of impeachment, the first stage of removing a president from office.

Members from either chamber can propose a bill.

There are no term limits for members.

THE SENATE

5 Every state, no matter the size of its population, is allotted _____ senators by the U.S. Constitution. There are 100 senators in total.

6 If the Senate is voting on a bill, and the result is split 50/50, the _____ casts the deciding vote.

7 A _____ becomes a law with majority support of both houses of Congress and the signature of the president.

8 A _____ majority vote is needed from both chambers of Congress to override a president's veto.

LEGISLATIVE BRANCH

This is the part where you get to write something about what you learned, saw, heard, or thought; so grab that pen and get going!

_____

_____

_____

_____

_____

_____

_____

_____

_____

_____

_____

_____

_____

_____

_____

_____

_____

_____

_____

_____

_____

_____

Answer Key:

1: Congress   **2:** Population   **3:** Speaker of the House   **4:** House of Representatives   **5:** Two   **6:** Vice President   **7:** Bill   **8:** Two-Thirds

THE STATES

scan here
to watch
this episode

THE STATES

In the United States, political powers are divided at the federal, state, and local levels. An American state is a political body that exists at the level below the federal and above the local governments.

When the American colonists declared independence in 1776, the 13 original colonies became the first 13 states under the Articles of Confederation. These states came under this confederation with a very limited national government, with each state acting similarly to an independent country. The states kept their own governing powers while also entering into a "firm league of friendship with each other, for their common defense, the security of their liberties, and their mutual and general welfare..."

When the Constitution was ratified in 1788, it created a nation with a new, more effective national government, but it also protected the powers of the states.

For example, the 10th Amendment asserts that if a power isn't listed in the Constitution, it belongs to the states or to the people. As a result, states retain considerable power over many issues, such as voting, taxation, and property. The Constitution also declares that new states can be added to the Union with approval from Congress. The grand total now equals 50 states, with Alaska and Hawaii the last to join in 1959.

THE STATES

Most state governments are organized similarly to the federal government with its three branches. For example, just as the president leads the Executive Branch in the federal government, governors lead the executive branches of the states. Each state has its own written constitution, outlining a structure of government that reflects the uniqueness of its people and culture. The United States is a large country with diverse populations, and the Founders believed that states are better able to handle the needs and issues of their residents rather than the federal government.

Today, the states across this nation still play a vital role in protecting the freedoms of citizens outlined in the Constitution.

FUN FACT:

The Massachusetts state constitution of 1780 is still in effect today, making it older than the federal constitution.

THE STATES

1 Just like the federal government, each state has its own governing document called a _____ that reflects the uniqueness of its people and culture.

2 States' rights exist in America because the _____ believed that they were better at handling the needs and issues of their residents than the federal government.

3 The 10th Amendment preserves states' autonomy by declaring that powers not given to the _____ government by the Constitution belong to the the people and the states.

4 During the Revolutionary War, the nation adopted the _____ in which the states entered into a "league of friendship" and maintained the ability to govern themselves.

5 The United States currently has ____ states, symbolized by the number of stars on our flag.

6 The last two states that joined the Union in 1959 were _____ and _____

7 Just as the president leads the Executive Branch in the federal government, the _____ leads the executive branch in state governments.

8 A new state must be _____ to join the Union.

THE STATES

This is the part where you get to write something about what you learned, saw, heard, or thought; so grab that pen and get going!

_____

_____

_____

_____

_____

_____

_____

_____

_____

_____

_____

_____

_____

_____

_____

_____

_____

_____

_____

_____

_____

Answer Key:

1: Constitution   **2:** Founding Fathers   **3:** Federal   **4:** Articles of Confederation   **5:** 50   **6:** Alaska and Hawaii

7: Governor   **8:** Approved by Congress

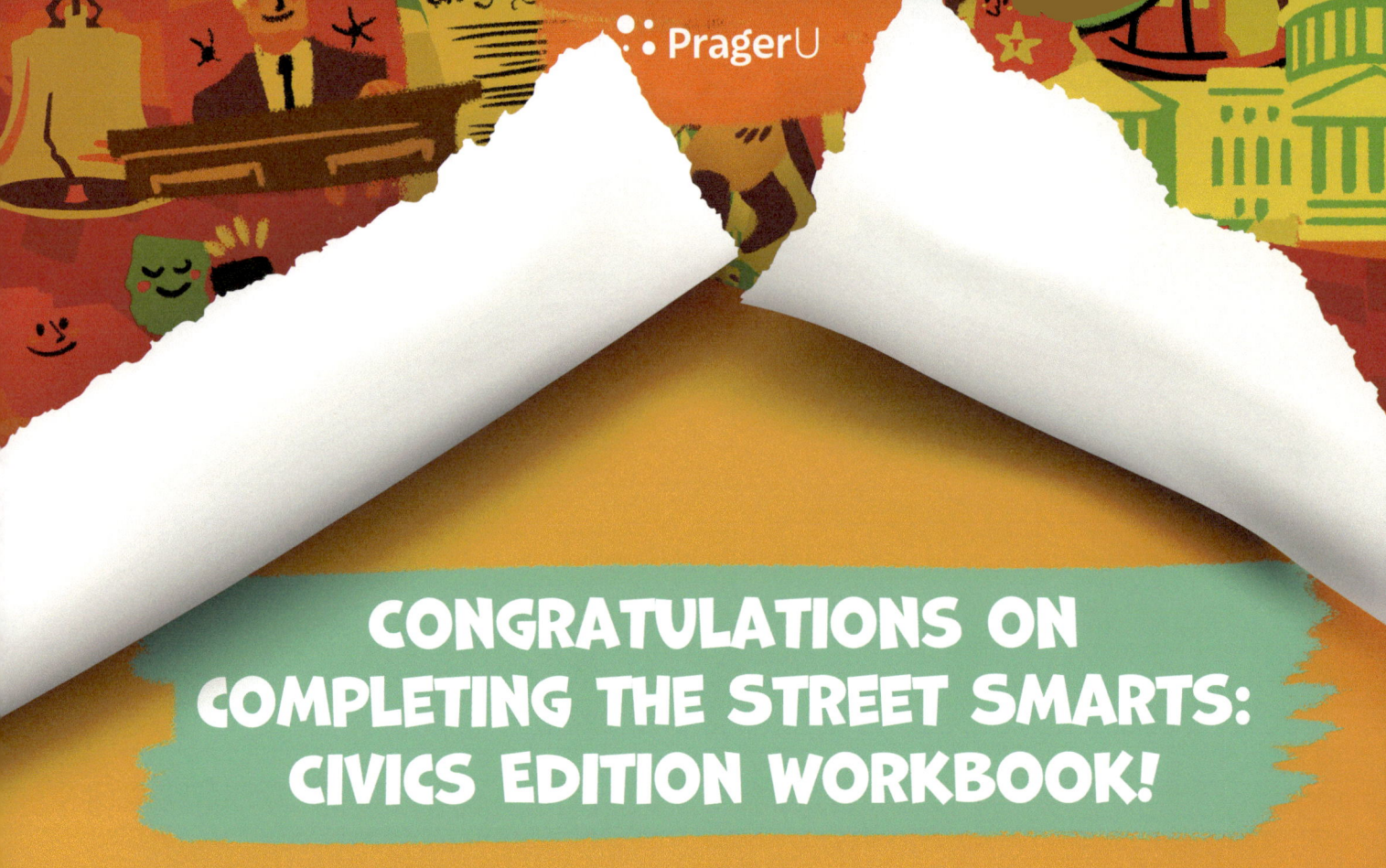

CONGRATULATIONS ON COMPLETING THE STREET SMARTS: CIVICS EDITION WORKBOOK!

Through this journey, you've covered the cornerstones of American Civics, strengthening your foundation as an informed and patriotic American citizen. Guided by Uncle Sam, you delved into the Declaration of Independence, understanding its pivotal role in our nation's history. Your studies then brought you to the U.S. Constitution, shedding light on the intentions of our Founding Fathers and the structure they established. The Bill of Rights was a key highlight, emphasizing the fundamental freedoms we hold dear. Your journey also took you through the Executive Branch's responsibilities, the Judiciary's role in our system of checks and balances, and the importance of the Legislative Branch in making laws that impact every American. Wrapping up, you gained insights into the importance of individual states and their rights within the Constitution. Each section of this workbook has contributed to a well-rounded understanding of our civic systems. Great job on your accomplishment!

WELL DONE!

NOTES

We're reaching America's youth with PragerU Kids!

With reliable and age-appropriate kids shows, books, and magazines that teach classic American values, PragerU Kids offers content that parents trust and children love. As a nonprofit, PragerU relies on the generosity of donors committed to helping us spread messages of liberty, economic freedom, and Judeo-Christian values to the next generation. PragerU Kids is the leading network that makes educational, entertaining, pro-American content for kids. Watch for free and learn more at:

PragerUkids.com

Made in United States
Troutdale, OR
09/14/2024

22823668R00026